Building the Blackfish

Building the Blackfish

Narrated by
DANA STORY

Photographs by
JOHN CLAYTON

Introduction by
PHILIP C. BOLGER

Ten Pound Island Book Company

Gloucester, Massachusetts

Copyright © 1988 by Dana Story.
All rights reserved. No portion of this book may be reproduced
without written permission of the copyright owner.

Library of Congress Card No. 88-50868

Distributed by International Marine Publishing Company,
Route 1, P.O. Box 220, Camden, Maine 04843.
ISBN 0-87742-980-4

Printed in the United States of America.

This book is dedicated to the memory of the Essex men who built Blackfish:

Jake Story
Leander Doucette
Steve Price
Phil Terrio
Dennis Martin
John Mulcahy
Ray Mulcahy
Pete Cogswell
Luther Burnham
Bob D'Entremont
Pete Hubbard
Sammy Gray
Charlie Andrews

Foreword

Shipbuilding was an industry which became established in what is now Essex, Massachusetts, back in the middle 1650's. The topography of the region, together with its soil characteristics, made it relatively inhospitable to agriculture on any large scale, so that, somewhat of necessity, the early settlers turned to the sea to augment their food supplies. Being blessed, however, with magnificent stands of virgin timber, of both hard and soft woods, they used these forests for lumber with which to build the boats employed in harvesting the sea. Thus was born a shipbuilding industry which grew to considerable prominence over the years. It reached a point where in the 1850's there were as many as sixteen shipyards in the little town, turning out over sixty vessels a year. Over the years it has been estimated that something in the neighborhood of 4,000 ships have come from the yards of Essex.

The building of a wooden ship, whether large or small, was a hand process, and with minor exceptions has remained so to the present day. In its nature it does not easily lend itself to mechanization, automation or prefabrication. As a hand process it was (and is) extremely interesting to watch, a fact attested by the hordes of people who, as automobiles and better roads became commonplace, stopped by the Essex yards to observe what was taking place.

One of those who came to Essex and was fascinated by the sights of an old-time shipyard was John Clayton, a man who had been brought up in Arkansas. Although hitherto unfamiliar with ships or shipbuilding, he was utterly captivated by the sights and sounds of the Essex shipyards—by the men, by what they were doing and how they did it. Being an able photographer and also one whose business was directly concerned with photography, he began to record in minute photographic detail the processes and operations by which a wooden ship was built. The result was a collection of many thousands of priceless and historic negatives which, as it turned out, also recorded the final years of the once great Essex shipbuilding industry.

John began this labor of love in 1937 when the only yard operating was that of Jacob Story, formerly the Arthur D. Story yard. Jake was just about to begin the construction of an 80 foot ketch-rigged auxiliary yacht, the *Skilligolee,* modelled somewhat after a Gloucester fishing vessel of the time. This John faithfully recorded, and before it was finished, a sweet little 52 foot schooner yacht was set up in the berth alongside the *Skilligolee.* John turned his attention and camera on this and produced several hundred negatives, taking them every few days from start to finish. From these he selected 100 and printed four sets of excellent 8 x 10s, putting them into splendid leather binders. One he gave to the owner, one to the architect, one to the builder and one for himself. A couple of years before he died, he presented me with his own copy which, as one might imagine, has become one of my most cherished possessions. This album, simply engraved "Blackfish", is the basis of our photographic narrative. It begins in March 1938 and ends on launching day, August 1.

The reader should bear in mind that while *Blackfish* was something of a special case, being quite small as Essex vessels went, and being a yacht with outside ballast, she nevertheless was built using the same general type of construction and with the same methods as hundreds of wooden schooners which preceded her in the Essex shipyards. The author (and no doubt many readers) wishes John had included a few more photos of the very early stages of the work, but we will try to deal with that as we deal with the pictures.

Finally, a few words of description concerning *Blackfish* may be in order. She was designed by naval architect Henry Scheel, one of his earliest commissions. The plans were worked up in the late fall and winter of 1937 - 38. She was actually 52 feet overall and very traditional in appearance. Her registered dimensions were: length 45.90 feet; breadth 13.60 feet; depth 6.90 feet; gross tons 18.00; net tons 17.00. Her framework was oak and her planking was yellow pine. The builder was Jacob Story of Essex, Massachusetts, who built her for Mendum B. Littlefield of Mamaroneck, New York. He was her only owner for all of the 25 years and two months of her life, which, so far as we know, was a pleasant one.

Blackfish was lost at approximately 5:15 a.m. on the morning of September 29, 1963 as she was on her way from Larchmont, New York to Greenport, Long Island for winter lay-up. Without the owner's realizing it, electrolysis had consumed the heads of the keel bolts, and at that moment the bolts pulled through the iron keel and it dropped off. The vessel rolled down and filled but did not wholly sink. All hands got off safely. Some time later she washed ashore. A Greenport boat builder paid $25 for the hulk and salvaged all that he could. The two lovely spars became flagpoles.

Dana Story
June 1988

Introduction

In 1813, the year the Story family took over the foreshore shown in this book, a gang of New York shipwrights trekked through the forest to Lake Erie, and began to fell trees. Between January and July they built a fort and several other large buildings, four barges, fourteen ships' boats, and seven warships including two 110 foot brigs mounting twenty-two guns each. Every part of the ships was built on the spot except the gun barrels and the sailcloth (spare a thought for the teamsters who got fifty or sixty cannon and forty thousand square feet of canvas across the wilderness). There were about two hundred shipwrights at the peak of production. In the fall their output blew the Royal Navy off the lake.

You see here what those men were like. This method of shipbuilding hardly changed between the sixteenth century and the 1940's when the last ships of that construction were built. The war effort rested on a mass production industry that launched fishing vessels and cargo carriers by the hundred. Gloucester alone took twenty-odd new vessels a year to replace shipwreck losses. Every winter the whole coast was littered with the wreckage of coasters and deep-water ships. The losses were replaced from yards like this one; bare shores. The capital was men, trained and self-equipped from boyhood. Almost every man shown in these photos was capable of designing and building a good ship without management.

The end was in sight as these pictures were made. Less trade travelled in small ships. Engines made shipwreck a rarity. Big ship timber no longer stood handy in mass production quantity. The descendants of these men build trucks and aircraft, elsewhere, with less hardship, maybe, but no more efficiently.

Philip C. Bolger
February 1988

Building the Blackfish

March 24, 1938

Traditionally, the beginning of a wooden ship comes with the laying of the keel. This is what we see here. However, this operation is not really the beginning; first of all, obviously, a naval architect draws a set of plans. Next, a loftsman takes those lines and drawings and enlarges them full size upon the loft floor. From these he makes a set of templates, or molds as we called them, by which the actual timbers are cut. In the case of our little schooner, yet one more step was required, and that was to make a wooden pattern for the casting of the 10 1/2 ton gray iron keel, unique, we think, among all Essex-constructed vessels. The keel was cast in halves, and here we see it in the process of being fastened to the 8 inch oak keel which would be above it and which would become a part of the "backbone" of the vessel. Notice a section of the keel mold lying on top of it. The L-shaped object in the foreground is the lower end of an enormous C-clamp. The two halves of the iron were joined in a 3 foot 6 inch scarf joint and the whole iron keel was fastened to the oak with 17 7/8 inch diameter bolts. Judging by the photograph they appear to be galvanized iron. The specifications didn't say.

March 25, 1938

In a photograph taken the next day, we see the completed keel, iron and wood, as it lies waiting to be rolled up. It has been assembled on its side simply because it would have been impossible to do it otherwise. Lying on top of it is the whole of the keel mold including deadwood, strongback and stern post. The timbers on the ground in front have nothing to do with "Blackfish".

March 19, 1938

To tell our story a little better, we hope, we have upset the chronology somewhat to show the assembling of a frame. Most people called them "ribs" but to us they were always "frames". Because they were so small and light (at least in comparison to one of our big vessels) the frames of "Blackfish" were assembled on a platform off to the side while the construction of the keel was going on. As they were finished, they were stacked up out of the way.

We see here how the parts which have been sawed out on the bandsaw are laid out and "dogged" into place. The man stooping over on the left seems to be carefully relating those pieces to the mold of that frame which lies on top. We can also plainly see the centerline string stretched out.

It's too bad we have to have all those spectators in the picture.

March 25, 1938

We see here a typical frame which has been assembled from its many component parts and is ready to be put in place. The various parts are known as futtocks, each having its own name and each carefully sawed to shape on the band saw. In this case the parts are bolted together with galvanized screw bolts, although in the bigger vessels frames were fastened together with locust trunnels. The specifications for "Blackfish" called for the framing stock to be oak, 3 inches thick, but unless we miss our guess, the stock being used here is thicker than that. In the background is a pile of freshly sawn pieces waiting to be assembled. The frame in the photograph is what is known as a "square frame", that is, a complete structural unit from side to side. "Blackfish" had 14 square frames spaced 15 inches on centers. When finished, the square frames were picked up bodily by the men and set in their proper places.

Sharp eyes will notice a juice running out between the layers of the frame. This was one of the early applications of Cuprinol and was used throughout the structure on all joined surfaces.

March 25, 1938

We meet here the first of several shipwrights we will encounter in the course of our story. Leander Doucette is using his adze, probably one of the most basic of all shipwrights' tools, to shape what will become the lower end of the vessel's stem. Another adze is lying in the chips. The form of the piece has been roughed out on the big bandsaw and Leander is bringing it to its finished dimensions. He could split a pencil mark with his adze and his finished surface was like glass. Beside his right leg is a standard two foot folding rule, an item in all shipyard pockets. If the turn-up on the legs is any indication, Leander has on a brand new pair of overalls which Mrs. Doucette hasn't yet had time to shorten.

Projecting into the right background is the bow of the 90 foot yacht "Skilligolee" entering her final stages of construction.

April 1, 1938

The keel has been rolled up and put in place. From here on the vessel will grow on top of it. Already we see the lower elements of the stem, one of which we saw Leander Doucette working on. That big keel mold is tacked into place to locate the stern structure.

Those stacks of blocks on top of the keel are something of a conundrum. Our first picture would seem to show that the keel bolts were deliberately made too long, although why we can only guess. Maybe by stacking wood on top of them and then cinching down the nuts, they may have been of assistance, somehow, in rolling up the keel. Then again, it may have been planned to put square frames and keelson down over them. This seems more likely.

April 5, 1938

Here we are again, four days later. We see the rest of the stem held now by its permanent shores. Aft, the stern post is in place.

The pipe fittings on the ground are the exhaust line for "Skilligolee". The bull fiddle hanging on the stage pole is pure whimsey.

April 16, 1938

We have discussed the definition and assembling of square frames. These form the central body of the ship. As the shape of the hull becomes finer and somewhat more complex at the bow and stern, the frames are erected in halves, one side at a time. These frames, whether at the forward or after end of the vessel, are called "cants". This is because in the early years of wooden shipbuilding they were "canted", or set at an angle to the centerline of the keel.

In this picture the keel and stem have been assembled, part of the stern structure is up, the square frames are in place and the keelson is finished. This, by the way, was not oak, but was 5 inch thick hard pine.

It is time now to erect the forward cants. Banging away with his adze as he trims the stem in preparation for raising the forward cants is John Mulcahy, another master shipwright of the old tradition. We would guess that the man below him, partly hidden by the staging, is probably cutting the rabbet. That long piece which connects the tops of the square frames with the stem is called a "harpen" and it supports and aligns the tops of the cants as they are raised.

April 21, 1938

Building the bow of a vessel is easy compared with building the stern. As is obvious, there's a lot more to building the stern. Here is an overview from the deck of "Skilligolee" nearing completion alongside. We see the elements of the backbone as they come to the form of the transom. Once the framing of the transom is in place, the after cants can then be put up.

It's impressive to see the extent and complexity of the staging necessary to do all of this.

April 23, 1938

Here is a good broadside view of the little schooner as her form begins to emerge. We see that all the forward cants are in place and work is progressing on the after structure. We see also that a good start is being made on the construction of the transom. That no men show in the picture leads us to bet that Jake Story, the builder, is "borrowing" them to lend a quick hand on the "Skilligolee", the framework of whose pilot house shows over "Blackfish", and which was due to launch in about ten days from the date of this picture. A couple of assembled after cants show at the right of the heap of trash.

April 23, 1938

This is how the keel looked when in place. On top of those two mighty hunks of iron, all 21,000 pounds of them, is the 8 inch keel and on top of that are the heels of the frames. The props against the keel we called "dog shores". The methods used to handle that iron keel and stand it in place were closely akin to those used to build the pyramids. To the best of our knowledge, this was the only Essex vessel to be built with outside ballast. The heavy timbers on which the keel rests will form part of the launching cradle when the day comes.

April 23, 1938

Here we see the basics of the stern structure. Slanting up from the keel to the transom is the strongback (or horn timber, if you will) supported by the stern post. The triangle thus created will be filled in with tapering pieces to form the dead wood. The last three square frames are standing on the strongback.

To erect the after cants will require four harpens, two on each side. We see that the two lower ones are already in place. The three principal elements of the transom are in place, but the presence of those "dogs" tells us they are not yet completely fastened. By the way, those heavy pieces of transom, known as vee-timbers, have been deliberately made too big. The reason for this will become apparent later on. Note that a framework or jig of sorts has been built to hold them in place temporarily.

April 30, 1938

A splendid view of the lower and after end of the keel showing the heel of the stern post and the keel fillers. We see how the strongback begins and how the square frames are mortised into it. The block under that left hand square frame tells us that the layout of the strongback was changed. Its presence, however, in no way compromises the strength of the ship. Note that a mold is being used for something in the opening, perhaps to lay out the centerline of the propeller shaft. Don't worry about that black knot. A graving piece will go in there.

May 4, 1938

Here's a nice view of the stem and the forward cants—all in place where they belong. The temporary pieces that hold them there are called ribbands. The heels of the cants are fastened off with four heavy galvanized ship spikes, probably 3/8 inch square and 5 or 6 inches long. We see the scarf joints of the various pieces and note that all surfaces are well saturated with Cuprinol. Note also that the rabbet is cut into the stem and is ready to receive the ends of the planks. Those long forward parts of the first cants will later become part of the fillers which will solidly block in the space between themselves and the stem. Chalk marked B's indicate fastenings. Oh yes, and that black batten tacked on there locates the sheer line.

Unfortunately we don't have a photograph which shows it, but suffice it to say that the after cants are essentially put up and fastened off in the same way except that each foot is also held with a mortise and tenon.

May 4, 1938

This photograph portrays a major step in the evolution of a curved transom stern, something of a trademark of Essex vessels. Though very early in the vessel's construction, and though the hull planking is only about to start, the transom is planked now for three reasons:

1. Sooner or later it has to be done anyway.
2. It gives the transom its structural integrity and rigidity.
3. Because the wood ends of the planking on the transom and the planking of the hull must be mitered where they meet, it is easier and better if the transom is done first

The transom planks were pre-bent in a jig. Notice the presence of the black sheer batten. We saw the forward end of it in the last picture. The bottom edge of it is the line.

May 7, 1938

The skeleton of the ship is now essentially complete and it is time to begin planking. Here we see the 2 inch oak garboard in place and we see how it was fastened. The plans don't specify, but in all probability the fastenings were 3/8 inch galvanized ship's spikes. (They might have been round or square.) Depending on where they were used, they could have been 4, 5 or even 6 inches long. Regardless of what the rest of the planking would be, oak was generally used for garboards because of its strength and toughness. (We have seen an oak plank twisted almost 90 degrees.) The after end of this plank was probably steamed as the ends of the two or three streaks above it would have been. Note that the end of the plank has been nibbed to avoid having it run off to a "shim point". The chalk line showing on the frames above was put there by the dubber as he trimmed the frames in preparation for the next streak of plank.

May 7, 1938

Let's leave the "academics" for a bit and just enjoy the composition of this nice photograph; the symmetry of frames viewed through the cross-pawls; the budding of the beautiful elms we used to have; the houses along Main Street; the little pear tree all in bloom at the right. What a lovely place to have a shipyard.

May 11, 1938

She has four streaks on now. "Streak" (also referred to sometimes as "strakes") means a single strip of plank around the boat. The plank being used is 2 inch long leaf yellow pine. We always called it hard pine. Some call it pitch pine. It was good planking because it was indeed hard and was very strong. It also came in long lengths, and the pitch or resin in it was repugnant to insects and resistant to rot. It did tend to split more easily than oak and would therefore not twist as well. A hard pine splinter in the hand would fester very quickly.

John Clayton's camera case rests in the immediate foreground. For those who are interested, he used a 4 x 5 inch R. B. Auto-Graflex to make most of these pictures. He usually carried an assortment of Cooke and Taylor-Hobson lenses for it. Seven of our photos were made with a 35 mm. series E Leica.

May 11, 1938

A close-up view of the scene in the previous picture. Immediately apparent is the difference in grain and appearance of the oak garboard and the hard pine planks above it. We see also that the first three streaks are nibbed. Whoever is lining plank is doing a good job because that streak's edge is as fair as can be. "Lining" plank means to calculate and then delineate the shape of each plank. It is a very important and critical job. The appearance of a finished hull is dependent in no small measure on how well the liner has done his job. The shape of "Blackfish" made for an easy hull to plank.

The chalk marks on the forward end of the keel show where a piece will be cut out and a proper fairing piece or "gump" put in rather than having just a little piece of "gingerbread" as would otherwise be the case. If you're wondering about that broad flat face of the stem, be assured that it will all be trimmed and faired by the time she hits the water.

May 11,1938

John Clayton's photograph is telling its own story much better than we could possibly hope to do. It's a wonderful composition too. Enough said.

May 11, 1938

We like this picture because it puts the schooner in splendid context with its surroundings. It sits, embraced by all its staging, on the banks of the lovely little Essex River into which literally thousands of wooden vessels have been launched beginning in the 1650's. Though called a river, it is actually only a tidal estuary which winds among hundreds of acres of salt marshes on the way to Ipswich Bay and the Atlantic Ocean. Obviously it is low tide at the moment. In the distance we see houses on Water Street in South Essex. The banks of the Essex River were lined with shipyards in the middle 1800's and the yard where "Blackfish" sits has been in continual use since before 1668.

May 14, 1938

Here is Phil Terrio dubbing the vessel. (His name was really Theriault, but he Anglicized it.) Although we touched upon it briefly earlier, we want to elaborate a little more on what Phil is doing here. Before any plank is hung onto a vessel, a small flat place has to be trimmed or "dubbed" with an adze from the curvature of each frame. This of course, is to allow the plank to lie flat and securely against the frame. These frames on "Blackfish" are small and the dubbing is relatively easy in contradistinction, shall we say, to those on a 140 footer with frames maybe 16 inches thick. It took arms of iron to do this all day long.

May 14, 1938

You can see that in our shipyard we didn't worry much about the clutter of odds and ends upon the ground. Trash wood generally stayed where it landed until the occasional day of clean-up. Nowadays a liability insurance inspector would cancel the policy if he saw a mess like this. Anyway, we do see the gang hanging the after plank of streak number 7. Note that on this they are fastening off the butt at the transom first and working forward. Remember that we spoke about that butt as being mitred.

The leaves are showing now on the big elm tree.

May 14, 1938

Here is a closer look at the gang hanging that plank. Steve Price (in felt hat), Ray Mulcahy and Leander Doucette are giving their undivided attention. Perhaps the streak's edge needs to be trimmed a little. Bob D'Entremont at left isn't just standing there—he's holding the plank against his chest. Bob is the sawyer and it is he who is roughing out all the planks on the bandsaw. From the bandsaw, planks go first to the beveler who puts the proper edges on them so that they will fit correctly against adjacent streaks.

May 14, 1938

Once again we have a photograph which pretty much speaks for itself. As the streaks rise up the stem we see that they no longer need to be nibbed. We see, also, that on these frames, at least, not much dubbing was needed. Phil Terrio's adze and a bucket of Cuprinol rest on the far stage.

May 21, 1938

We have seen two or three times what the wood ends at the bow looked like. Now we see in fine fashion what they looked like at the stern. We see the mitred butts and we see what an impressive amount of wood is trimmed off the vee-timbers. Much more will come off before we're through. Heavy shores are now in place to give adequate support to the whole stern.

Strictly speaking this is not a "wineglass" transom since there will not be that little pointed projection at the center of the bottom.

May 21, 1938

From seven streaks on May 14 we've gone to thirteen on May 21. Not counting Sunday, that's a streak a day—good, but by no means exceptional. In years past, two streaks a day around a big vessel was not unusual. Again we see that very little dubbing seems to be required, which tells us the loftsman did a good job, the man who molded the timber did a good job and that the frames were assembled and placed with care.

The guide string which the dubber is using is just visible aft.

May 24, 1938

Planking the outside of a ship was hardly more than half the battle. The inside had to be planked too. Inside planking is known as "ceiling" (why it isn't "sealing" we don't know) and putting it in was nearly as laborious, although perhaps not as painstaking, as hanging the outside planking. You slipped and skidded as you worked and it always seemed as if the staging was too low (or too high). It was something of a challenge to see how far up the sides the ceiling could be installed before building a stage at all. Furthermore, all those heavy planks had to be passed in over the side of the ship.

Anyway here are the first pieces of ceiling going into "Blackfish".

June 1, 1938

Look at that! She's a boat now! From a labor standpoint, however, she isn't even half done. The fillers and knightheads have gone into the bow and chalk marks locate bowsprit and hawse pipes although it will be a while yet before they show up. The sight of Cuprinol running out the plank seams spells trouble and aggravation for the caulker. It's a devil of a job to caulk with stuff like that in a seam.

June 4, 1938

This is the shop and the mill and the working area in front. "Mill" was the name we applied to the building which housed the big band saw. It also contained an ancient surface planer, the lathe for turning trunnels and a splendid big old wet stone. It was an exciting place when the machinery was turning. The noise of the whirling pulleys, flapping belts, and whining saw were friendly sounds. One somehow didn't even mind the scream of the planer. Perhaps the nicest thing about it was the wonderful smell of fresh chips and sawdust. There's a kind of reassurance in making things out of wood.

Here we see Bob D'Entremont, John Mulcahy and Steve Price as they contemplate a piece of ceiling before sawing it. To the left, Phil Terrio, having finished with the dubbing, is now getting out stanchions.

June 4, 1938

The stanchion Phil was working on is about done and here he applies the sandpaper to smooth it up. Stanchions are those timbers which project above the deck to which the bulwarks and rail-caps are attached. Note the well worn oil stone and two smoothing planes—wooden, of course. We see also the traditional carpenter's hand toolbox used in similar form by probably every ship carpenter. They kept their complete collection of tools in their big chests stored in the shop. The tools expected to be used for the day were carried to the job in the hand box.

June 4, 1938

Here we again see Steve Price, John Mulcahy and Bob D'Ent bending in the piece of ceiling they were getting ready to saw out two pictures ago. In big ships it took special clamps called "ginneys" to do what John and Bob are here doing simply by leaning against the plank. The ceiling in "Blackfish" was fir, 1 3/4 inches thick. Obviously the ceiling cannot be completed until all stanchions are in.

June 4, 1938

Essentially the same scene as the previous picture but with emphasis on the port side. We have an excellent illustration of what the stanchions looked like and how they were put in. Ray Mulcahy works from the outside with Dennis Martin on the inside. It shows that when finished, the topsides of a vessel are quite solidly filled in with timber.

The fellows on the other side are still struggling with that piece of ceiling.

June 4, 1938

We've just seen what was going on inside the boat; now we see what it is looking like on the outside. Note the ribband to hold the tops of the stanchions and the chalk marks along the sheer streak to indicate where the stanchions would go.

A real post card setting is created in the photograph. At the time it was taken, Jacob Story was the fourth generation of his family to build ships on this spot going back to 1813. It is adjacent to common land which was set aside by the town government in 1668 "for a yard to build vessels and to employ workmen for that end."

June 6, 1938

Here we again get a look at the transom now that the planking is done. The fairing (chopping?) that's been done on the vee-timber nearest us shows why it had to be so big in the first place. We also see by the spike heads how the stanchions were fastened and we note with interest that the top edge of the sheer streak is painted black. This is because it makes it much easier for the builder to stand off and sight it for fairness if it's black.

June 12, 1938

If you've been waiting to see how that big open triangle at the stern was filled in, here's your answer. It does indeed have a rough and crude look, but later on another photo will show how it all faired in beautifully. We see the strongback emerging from the rabbet; we see the stern post which will not have to be trimmed significantly; we see the chalk marks indicating the location of fastenings; we see where the shaft hole will be. Manifestly there will be no shaft log as such. Rather, there will be a hole, the diameter of which is indicated and which, in all probability, will be lined with a lead sleeve bedded in white lead. Lastly, we see that much of the after end of the vessel has been caulked since the seams that show have already been puttied.

A careful comparison of these photographs with the architect's plans reveals that Jacob Story made a number of modifications and alterations to the plans and specs presumably based on his extensive experience. In a number of cases scantlings (dimensions) were increased and timber layouts adjusted, wisely in our judgement.

June 12, 1938

We can hardly see the little girl, encased in staging as she is. The time has come now to finish up the structure of the transom. First of all, it will take seven standing timbers of which we see that five are now in place. We will shortly see how the rest is done.

June 12, 1938

Look at all those spike heads that will have to be bunged. We're guessing that they're 3/4 inch diameter and we know they'll be white pine bungs. Sharp eyes will pick out five little cotton "tails" which the caulker has left to locate his work. It would appear that much of the bottom has been caulked. Seams like these probably had a thread of cotton on the bottom with a thread of oakum on top. A caulked seam would be payed with lead paint to bind the oakum before being puttied. ("Putty" is the generic term we used to indicate any type of seam compound.) The paint also served to help prevent the oils of the putty from leaching out. This looks like a good planking job. The streaks are narrow and the seams are small and uniform. She'll be relatively easy to smooth up.

June 12, 1938

See what has been accomplished since June 4 when we last looked inside. The ceiling is finished, the clamp is in, the shelf is in and we have a breasthook and five deck beams. Notice that a generous air space has been left between the top of the ceiling and the bottom edge of the clamp and that the ceiling stops considerably short of the keelson. This is to ensure a good circulation of air through the structure.

June 12, 1938

There's a lot of structural detail illustrated here. Most obvious is the landing of a deck beam upon clamp and shelf. The clamp was made up of two streaks of fir—the top one approximately 3 inches by 7 inches, the lower one approximately 2 1/2 inches by 6 inches. The photographs or drawings don't show whether the butts were scarfed. (If they weren't they should have been.) The shelf also was fir, two layers 3 inches by 3 inches. If you imagine the structure of a boat as something of a girder, it is the keel, keelson and garboards which give strength to the bottom, and the clamp, shelf and deck which give strength to the top. The clamp and shelf therefore are important structural members. Here we see the deck beam mortised into both clamp and shelf, something to which we would take exception. We see also the notches cut into the stanchions on which the covering board will rest.

June 18, 1938

The application of a coat of Cuprinol certainly brings out the grain in all that oak deck framing. What we see here is the framing on the starboard side of the main trunk cabin. Happily, the shelf isn't cut here because the shelf tilts down a little bit as it runs aft. We do see that the inboard ends of the carlings are dovetailed into the header. (What we in Essex called "carlings" were often referred to as "short beams" or "half beams" in other places.) There will be a tie-rod put in here and in other deck openings before the decking is laid. Smoothing of the framing and joints in preparation for this is already underway.

June 25, 1938

As far as deck framing is concerned, this photograph pretty well tells it all. Beginning aft, we see that the last upright piece of the transom is clamped into place. The "horse beam" shows in front of it. Coming forward, we see that the covering board is all installed, although whether or not the stanchions have been pined we can't tell. Vis-a-vis the deck framing, we see the lodging knees, the tie rods at the openings, the main mast partners and we see that main beams forward and aft of each deck opening have been doubled. Around the perimeter of the deck, we see the little filler blocks put between the beams as landing for the decking. Close inspection shows that they're not all in yet on the port side.

Those oak pieces running down the centerline are the first of two streaks of what we called the "king plank" and in fact are the first pieces of decking. The rest of the decking is laid outward from these.

June 25, 1938

The work may often be hard and heavy, but it needn't be unpleasant or unduly taxing when there is an easy camaraderie and friendly rapport among those doing it, as, for example, in this picture. Here we see Leander Doucette and Dennis Martin, both natives of Nova Scotia or "down home" (the terms were synonymous). They're spiking down a section of king plank and appear to be having a pleasant time. Of course, we might add that anybody who worked with Leander Doucette had a good time, and that plenty of laughter was an integral part of life in the Essex shipyards.

June 30, 1938

And here is the deck being laid outward, as we said, from the king planks. We see it as it comes into the nibbing streak which, in turn, lies against the covering board. We have a good look, too, of the way in which the decking is squeezed together before spiking. We suspect that may be Dennis Martin working beside the forward companionway with its curved slide and round deadlights. An interesting assortment of tools lie on deck.

July 2, 1938

A considerable change has taken place in the appearance of "Blackfish" since last we saw the outside. It's our guess that the town clock has just struck twelve and the gang is starting home for dinner (not lunch). Ray Mulcahy is just coming over the rail while Steve Price finishes tapping in one last piece of pine shim around that stanchion.

July 2, 1938

Sure enough, the gang has gone home for dinner and left tools and stuff lying right where they were. It's almost axiomatic that as soon as any decking is laid, a mess appears on it. It's a good view, though, of the laying of the deck and the beginnings of the various deck structures. Forward is the forecastle companionway; next we see a skylight and in the foreground is the opening for the cabin trunk. The decking is 2 inch by 2 inch fir probably dressed to 1 3/4 inch by 1 3/4 inch. Traditionally decking was white pine although fir was sometimes used.

We can see three hand toolboxes sitting around and the handles of two more, albeit many of the tools seem to be lying on the deck. Parked in the driveway is a '34 Packard and a '30 Model A Ford.

July 2, 1938

After taking the previous picture, John Clayton went forward and took this one looking aft. (Or maybe it was the other way around.) He managed to catch builder Jake Story just as he was about to go over the side. Anyway, the mess is just as impressive in either direction. Note the blueprint of the construction plan tacked to the piece of plywood lying by the starboard rail.

July 2, 1938

Except to call attention to the after end of the covering board sticking out over the sheer streak, there isn't much we can say about this photograph that it doesn't say for itself. It might be mentioned that old-timers in the Essex yards referred to the covering board as the "planksheer".

July 6, 1938

We're getting there! The bowsprit, lying on a couple of sawhorses, is waiting to go in. The foot-rails clearly show as does the grain of the Douglas fir. In all probability, this bowsprit and the rest of the spars were made in the spar yard of Charles H. Andrews across the street from the shipyard out back of the barbershop.

July 6, 1938

A close-up of the after skylight, just ahead of the cockpit. It's made of white pine as were all skylights. Across the river are the remains of "Corporation Wharf", used for generations as a shipyard by a number of Essex builders, the last being Moses Adams. After him it was used for timber storage by the Tarr and James yard.

July 9, 1938

John Mulcahy and the skipper confer about the placement of the starboard hawsepipe. John's rule and pencil are immediately available in his shirt pocket.

In the interval between the taking of this picture and the next one, someone will have sawed off the port knighthead.

July 9, 1938

Note:

1. Bowsprit is in
2. Knighthead and stanchions are sawed off
3. Forward deck is all laid
4. Forward deck is partly caulked (tails sticking out)
5. The nibbing streak (strake?) at edge of deck
6. The king planks
7. Hole for the mainmast partly cut
8. Forecastle companionway about finished
9. Door for same
10. It's dinnertime again
11. 1934 Packard
12. 1937 Ford

(John Clayton was very sensitive about getting in the way or bothering the men and took pains to avoid it. Thus, many of his pictures were taken in the noon hour.)

July 9, 1938

Same day, same time.

Again note:

    1. Main cabin skylight
    2. Quarter bitts are in
    3. After deck is all laid
    4. Luther Burnham caulking deck
    5. It's high tide for a change

Luther is working just now for two reasons: first, as caulker, he came and went as needed; secondly, it was difficult to caulk the deck while the gang were working on it, so he took advantage of the noon hour to get as much done as he could while they were gone. Because he lived in Essex Falls and walked wherever he went, he brought his dinner with him.

July 9, 1938

Luther Burnham began work as a caulker in 1912 at the age of 21. His father, a lifelong caulker, taught him the trade and he never did anything else in the shipyard. He never married and lived alone in the family home. He was thought of by all as a real "character". Here, with black mesquite mallet in hand, he works on the after deck. We're not sure why he has that bit of oakum there.

July 9, 1938

The gang has come back from dinner and are again hard at work. John Mulcahy walks aft, Pete Cogswell (in straw boater) bends to the finishing touches on the companionway and Leander Doucette, with mallet and gouge, is cutting the mast hole. The hand box with the fancy handle belongs to Pete, a finish carpenter, or, as we called them, an inboard joiner.

July 9, 1938

Leander has come below, presumably to finish the mast hole from the under side. He's using a bung bit to make small starting holes for a regular long barefoot augur. Behind him is the matched pine of the forecastle bulkhead, one of two structural bulkheads in the boat. She did, however have 14 pairs of what would be considered hanging knees. These were not wooden knees in the usual sense of the word, but were instead wrought iron angle straps fitted to beams, shelf and clamp. The thickness varied from tips to throat.

July 9, 1938

We can't see what he's doing, but the skipper is obviously intent upon something. "Blackfish" even has some topside paint now.

July 16, 1938

The railcaps are going on. The specs called for teak, 2 inches by 6 inches, but we can't tell from the photographs whether it is, in fact, teak. We see, too, that the hawsepipes are in and that they're not the same, port and starboard. This is not a mistake, but rather is occasioned by the design of the windlass.

July 16, 1938

We've waited all this time to see how the transom is finished off. Here's Phil Terrio putting up the top outside pieces. Back to us, the figure on hands and knees is probably Sammy Gray puttying the deck. Forward, the skipper is busily puttering around, not doing any particular good, but having a fine time.

July 16, 1938

The assembling of the traditional curved elliptical transom stern is one of the things that separated the men from the boys as far as ship carpenters were concerned. It was a fussy, painstaking and laborious job, no doubt about it, and it was a hard and heavy job too as you can see from the sizes of the timber which went into it. If the oak timbers were this size for a 52 footer, imagine what they must have been for a big schooner.

Master of the situation is Phil Terrio in this splendid portrait. He's putting an auger in an old Black & Decker boring machine.

July 16, 1938

See? We told you that it would all come out right. That motley assortment of timber in the deadwood has all been polished off in fine fashion. The Cuprinol makes it look as if it had been varnished. Sharp eyes may be able to pick out the stopwaters in that timber through which the shaft runs. And maybe you didn't notice Ray Mulcahy lying on the ground under the keel as he works on the lower rudder fitting.

July 16, 1938

Putting on rail caps was no picnic either. They have to be molded to the shape of the hull, they have to be scarfed (as we see here) and they have to be mortised over the head of each stanchion. The function of the diagonals between stanchions under the rail cap forward is puzzling.

We have a good look at the structure of the cabin trunk, and we note that the after deck is caulked and puttied.

For the skipper to try to sweep the deck at this stage seems like an exercise in utter futility.

July 16, 1938

Seeing Pete Cogswell as he drives a bolt through the trunk side gives us a good look at how the cabin trunks were put together. The beams are oak, of course, and the sides are white pine, and they appear to be about 3 inches dressed to about 2 3/4 inches. They would have to be that much in order to let the beams in properly. It actually said on the construction drawing that the trunk side should "fall inward 1/2 a level bubble".

Notice that nicely turned mallet lying by Pete's foot.

July 16, 1938

A lot of things are happening. They'd have to be if "Blackfish" is to go overboard on time. There's Pete again in his straw boater and beside him Sammy Gray putties deck. At the left, Jake Story, in a fedora no less, gives some directions to Phil and Leander building the top of the transom. Maybe it's time to throw away that old broom in the foreground.

It's interesting to note that fifty years ago, men who worked outdoors in the summer were not the sun worshippers we have today. They wore shirts with underwear and they wore hats or caps.

July 24, 1938

We know it's Sunday because there's not a soul in sight and we can see the canvas pulled up over the stuff on deck. That two-wheeled dolly in the foreground was used to move heavy timbers around.

It is now July 24 and "Blackfish" would be launched on August 1. It is nothing short of amazing to see the amount of work that will be accomplished in those eight days one of which will be another Sunday.

July 24, 1938

The transom is finished and now awaits the rail cap. The inside planking appears to be oak. Note that the decking runs under it. In the middle, below, somewhat hidden by chips, is the blocking for the sheet snubber. The broad molded pieces of pine on either side of the transom, between it and the last stanchions, are fashion pieces necessitated by the tumble-home in the rails at the stern.

July 24, 1938

The nibbing streak on the starboard side aft. The deck will all be smoothed up before it is painted. This would not be done before launching, however.

July 24, 1938

The completed transom is shown from the outside. This conveys a good impression of how it all went together. Looking at the fashion piece from this angle, we see why it is necessary. Still to go on are the bulwarks and rail cap.

We've commented at length about the transom, but unquestionably it is the most complex part of a schooner and difficult to execute well.

July 24, 1938

The skeg from the starboard side; now we see the rudder. The rudder stock was bronze. Gudgeons and pintles have yet to be fitted. We also see a variable pitch propeller. No doubt the propeller shaft is held by a simple cutless bearing.

Originally the boat was designed to have the engine and shaft off center on the starboard side with a log coming through the counter. As construction started, it was moved to the centerline.

As we look at these photographs, we're prompted to wonder how many gallons of Cuprinol went into the boat. Here it's even bleeding out the stopwaters.

July 24, 1938

The "patent" windlass. As hard as we've tried, we can't make out the name cast into the end piece. The pieces of wood showing under it are only the shipping cradle. We wonder why all those hand augers are lying there. We know, however, that ship carpenters in 1938 didn't expect to bore every hole with a machine. Under the augers is one of the gammon irons. The pawl post will ultimately be sawed off.

That's a bruiser of a turnbuckle out there on the bobstay.

July 28, 1938

It's a "run for the roses" as you might say. Things are humping aboard the "Blackfish". We see the completed forward skylight, the deck mostly caulked and puttied, and canvas on the trunkstop. In the scuppers, we see the chain plates waiting for installation. Aft, the last pieces of rail cap are being put in place. Pete Cogswell works at the companionway with caulker Burnham beside him. (Those are two of the very oldest Essex names, dating back to the 1630's.)

That basket seems to be a fixture on deck.

July 28, 1938

As good a photograph of a caulker at work as we've ever seen. Luther Burnham was an exception among caulkers. He caulked decks working on his knees. Most caulkers sat on a little sliding combination seat and toolbox or else used a small folding stool that ran on wheels. Whether kneeling or wheeling, the tools were the same and so were the methods. A caulker's black mesquite (or live oak) mallet was practically an extension of his own right arm. Here we have a fine detail of a caulking mallet. We also see a caulker's reefing hook, chisel and bevelled iron.

Perhaps more than any other sound, the ringing blow of a caulker's mallet on the caulking iron told the town a ship was being built.

July 28, 1938

Installation of the steering gear and exhaust system. Piping and machine work was done by outside contractors and not the yard men.

July 28, 1938

Steve Price heads aft for something before starting on the last of the bulwarks. Just ahead of him we can see some of the scuppers cut into the waist.

July 28, 1938

Steve was well into his seventies when these pictures were made. This sprightly and vigorous little man was a ship carpenter of the highest order and was well able to turn his hand to any aspect of the work. Any younger man would do well to keep up with him.

Here Steve and someone we can't identify put the "shutter" in the bulwarks.

July 28, 1938

Sammy Gray is drawing the waterline as he puts on the last coat of copper paint before launching. Notice that the launchways are already under the vessel. Soon the cradle will be built, the staging and shores will come down and the bolt holes in the hull will be quickly plugged.

August 1, 1938

With the vessel going overboard, we've got to be able to steer her, so here we see the lovely mahogany wheel with those nice whitewood diamond inlays. We would suspect the steering gear to be an Edson although we can't really tell. The steering box still remains to be built as does the T-shaped cockpit. Beneath the starboard rail lies the sheet snubber.

That manila line on the quarter bitt is there in preparation for launching.

August 1, 1938

The tide's coming and it won't be long now. (Bob D'Ent and Sammy Gray could say the same about the cradle timber they're sawing off.) There's Steve again on the far side. Two of the most basic shipyard tools appear in the picture—the cross-cut saw and a 5 pound pin maul.

We get a good look at the launching cradle and the ways as they stretch down into the river.

August 1, 1938

At last! She's done—well, almost done. There is, in fact, still a lot of work remaining to be finished. There's deckwork including the cockpit, installation of various items of hardware and essentially all of the joiner work below deck. Also, of course, there's the spars and rigging and the installation of the engine. But the hull of "Blackfish" is finished and stands ready to be launched. Underneath, Phil Terrio and Steve Price busy themselves with ways and cradle while Leander Doucette, sitting on the bow in a remarkable likeness of Rodin's "The Thinker", contemplates where and how to make fast the snubbing line attached to the "drag". Bob D'Ent climbs the ladder on one last errand.

August 1, 1938

Because she was small with high bilges, it was easier to launch "Blackfish" in a cradle rather than using the "hell for leather" side launching common to the fishing schooners. Interestingly, the cradle method was also used on the largest and heaviest vessels we built ranging up to 800 gross tons.

The runners of the cradle (or sled if you will) are known as the "sliding ways" while the tracks down which the vessel slides are known as "ground ways". Before release, both sets of ways are clamped and/or bolted together at the upper end. To release the vessel it is only necessary to saw off the sliding ways just behind the place where they are fastened. Grease and gravity do the rest. A pair of men with a cross-cut saw on each side do the sawing, making sure as they go that both way ends will be severed at the same moment.

Here Pete Cogswell and Phil Terrio do the honors on the starboard side with Sammy and Bob D'Ent on the port side. The sponsor with her bottle of champagne awaits the "moment of truth".

August 1, 1938

Would you believe it? We don't have a photo of "Blackfish" hitting the water! Anyway, here she is immediately after that long and eagerly awaited moment, and she's floating exactly upon her designed waterline. All of that cradle stuff must be hauled ashore while some friendly people in outboard boats take her in tow for the old wharf at the James shipyard. The "crew" consists of Ray Mulcahy, Peter Hubbard, the author and John Mulcahy at the wheel. (John and Ray were father and son.)

August 1, 1938

Here's "Blackfish" viewed through the frames of the fishing vessel which came along behind her in the Jacob Story yard. An end and a beginning, a cycle repeated thousands of times in 330 years of Essex shipbuilding.

August 1, 1938

"Blackfish" heads around the bend on her way to the wharf. We see that the cradle has been hauled ashore, and in the foreground are the severed ends of the ways.

This lovely, gentle scene of the Essex River with the marshes, trees and uplands beyond is in stark and sad contrast to the scene today where a similar view would include much of two jerry-built marinas with their legions of garish plastic boats.

August 1, 1938

Phil Terrio is waiting for us as we tie up to the wharf. The butt of the mainmast is just behind him. Spoiling the composition, the author (aged 19) stands squarely in the middle.

August 1, 1938

In our last Essex picture, taken within an hour of launching, we see the riggers installing the foremast. They're using "shear poles" to do it, the method used in Essex for generations to hoist heavy objects. Builder Story (with pipe) watches with the rest of the gang.

Date Unknown

And at last we see what it all came to. Here's "Blackfish" in an excellent view shot on Long Island Sound with everything set except her fore topsail. From a distance, perhaps, we might easily imagine her to be one of the great Gloucester schooners.